MW00995737

# YONI MAGIC
# the Amazing Truth

My Little Yoni

MLY Press 2021

Copyright © 2021 by My Little Yoni, LLC

All Rights Reserved

First Printing 2020

Published by MLY Press
PO Box 232
Topanga, CA 90290

Printed in the United States

*No reader should consider the information in this book as a substitute for medical advice or for seeing a medical professional.*

www.MyLittleYoni.com

Whether you're a boy, girl, nonbinary person, or anything else*, you deserve to love and cherish your body.

*I will say girl, woman, and female today. However, not everyone with a Yoni identifies as a female. You can learn more in my book, 'Yoni Magic: Breaking the Binary.'

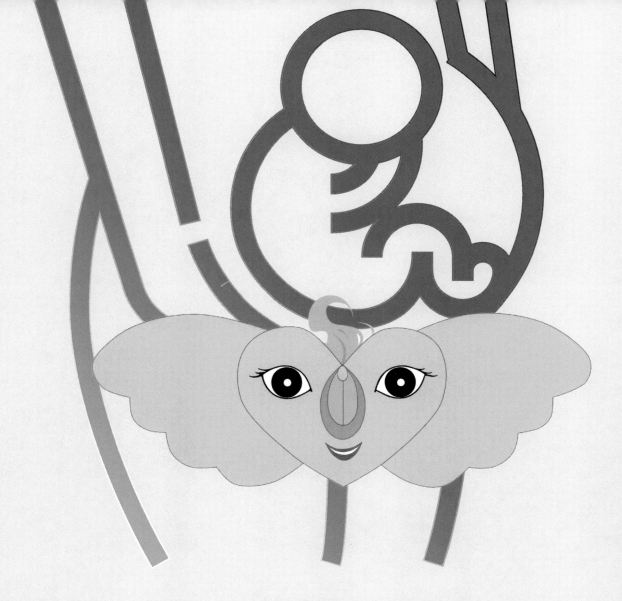

Babies come out of Yonis. Yoni is an ancient Sanskrit word for womb and **vulva** meaning 'sacred gateway.'

Sadly, there's still a lot of shame surrounding Yonis.

Many people don't know how to talk about Yonis or the miracle of making and birthing life.

Shame is a feeling of humiliation or distress. It's usually caused by messages from others that tell us we are somehow bad or wrong.

Shame Monster

Even if the messages are not true, shame can stick around and turn into a monster, repeating mean, untrue, things inside your head!

While shame can start out small, left unchecked, it can grow into bigger shame monsters and spread to others!

Your external genitals are called your vulva. But there's more to assigned female (AFAB) anatomy than what's on the outside!

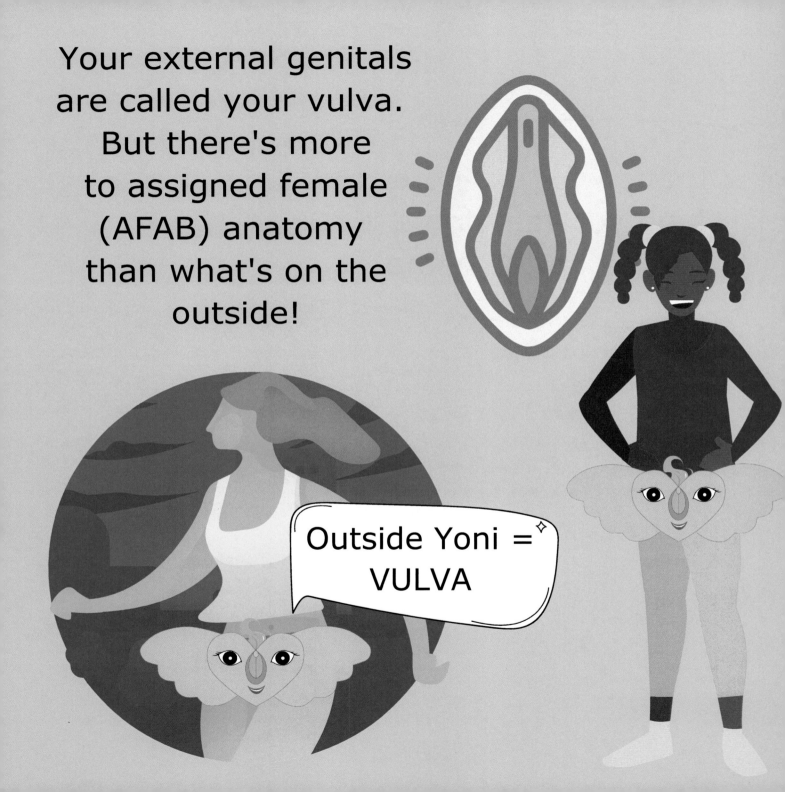

Outside Yoni = VULVA

Inside of the body, Yoni includes the entire reproductive system of a woman, such as the **uterus** or womb where a baby grows before it's born.

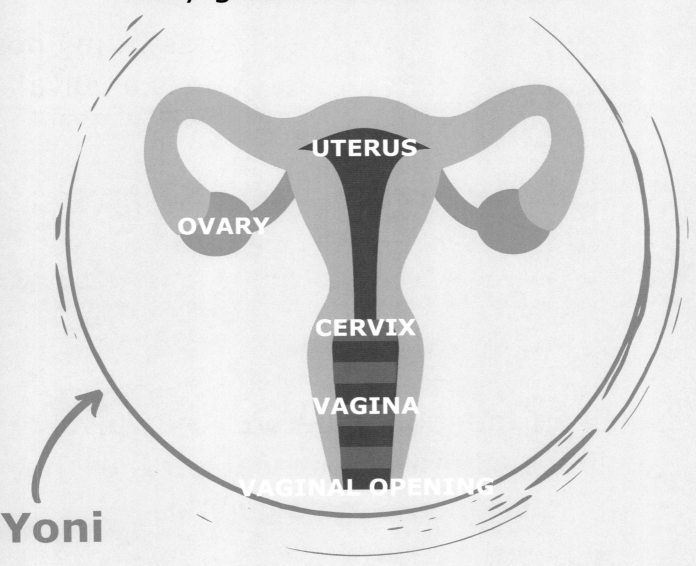

It's important to know accurate anatomical terms for Yonis.

Like I mentioned before, the vulva includes all of the external parts of the assigned female genitals.

Up at the top of the vulva is the visible part of the **clitoris.**

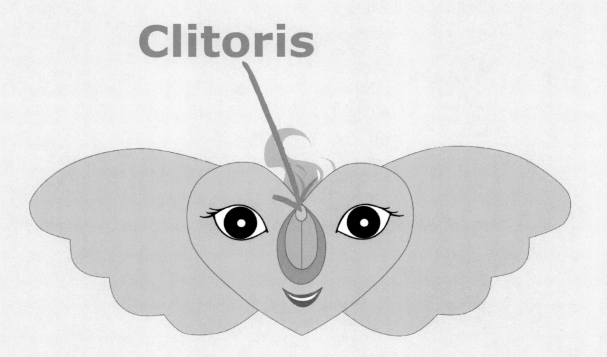

Clitoris

The clitoris has 8,000 nerve endings in it, making it one of the most sensitive parts of the female body!

You know when you get tickled and feel all those strong sensations in your body?

That's because signals travel from the **nerves** in your armpits to your **brain**, creating a strong sensation.

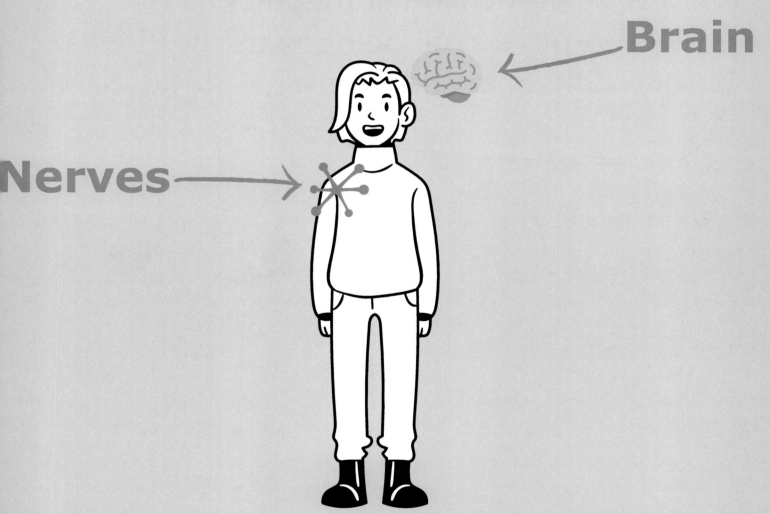

**NEVER** touch someone's Yoni without permission.* (Another word for permission is consent.) **ALWAYS** treat Yonis with kindness & respect.

This will keep me and other Yonis happy & safe!

*to learn more about this vital subject, read my book 'Yoni Magic: All about Consent'

Now let's talk about the 'lips' of the Yoni.

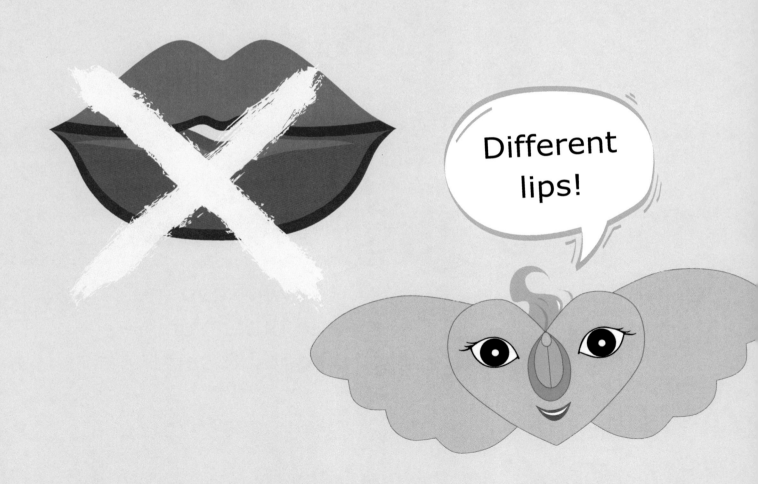

Over here is the **labia majora**. Their job is to protect all the external parts of the vulva.

Labia
Majora

They protect the yoni from dirt or other things that could cause infection.

Inside the labia majora
are the **labia minora**.

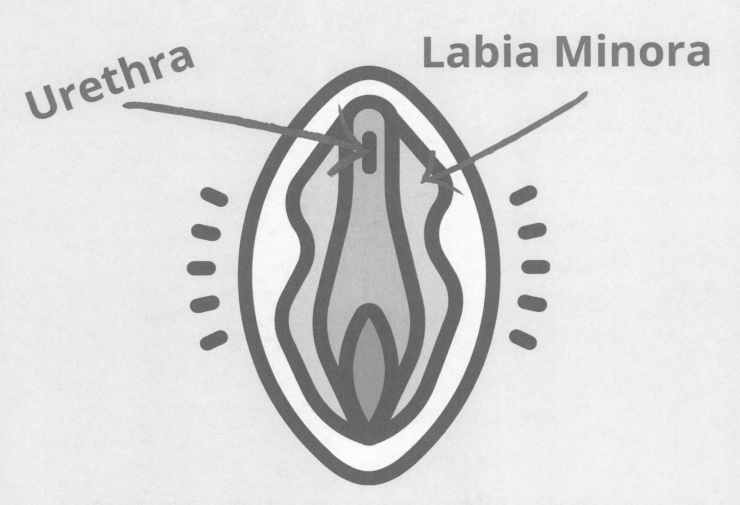

Urethra

Labia Minora

They surround the opening to the
urethra, where pee comes out.

The **vagina** is a muscular canal that connects the uterus to the outside world. This is the birth canal, where vaginally birthed babies come out.

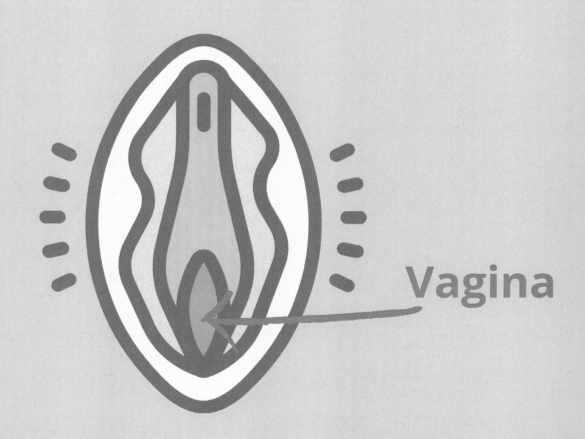

Vagina

Remember I mentioned the clitoris earlier? Well, most of it is inside! The internal portions of the clitoris wrap around the urethra and extend to the top of the vagina.

**Internal Clitoris**

The internal clitoris holds the erectile tissue, increases lubrication in the vagina, and increases sensation.

As a super hero from the Yoniverse,
I look quite different than human
vulvas on Earth.

You Are Here

Every woman's vulva is different in size, shape, color, and pubic hair but ALL vulvas are uniquely beautiful!

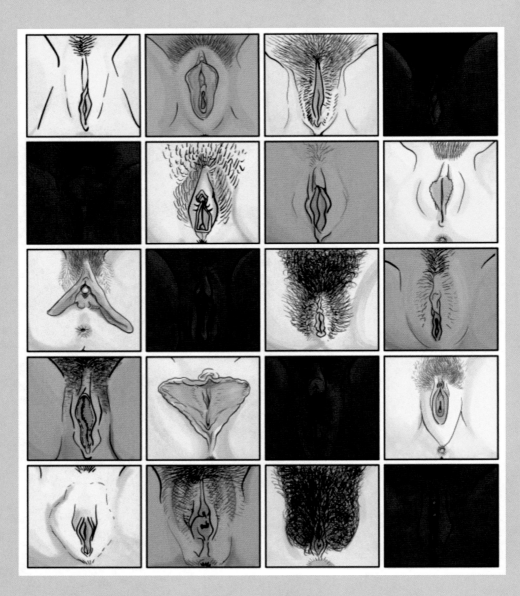

Remember I mentioned before that babies come from Yonis?

Well, babies can come to their parents in different ways including adoption, surgically born babies, or vaginally birthed babies.

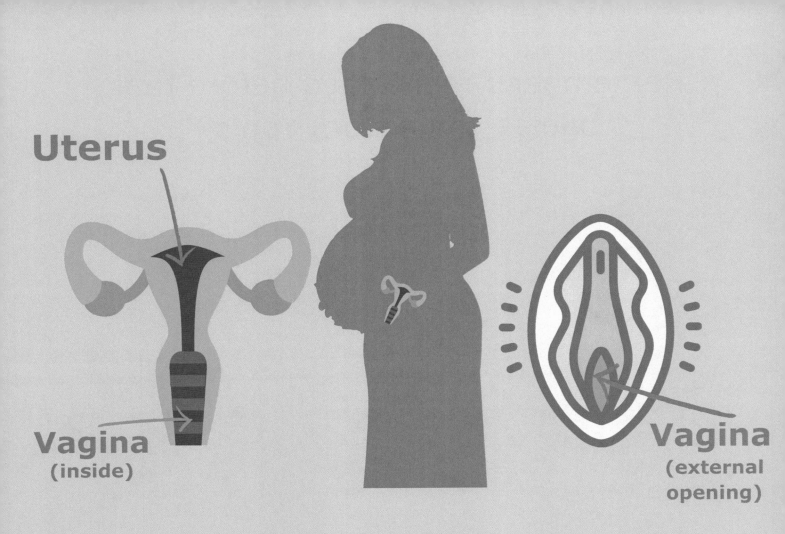

**Uterus**

**Vagina**
(inside)

**Vagina**
(external opening)

In a vaginal birth, a baby travels from the uterus out through the vagina. Can you see why Yoni means 'sacred gateway'? You can thank Yonis for the gift of life!

Now that you've learned
more about Yonis...

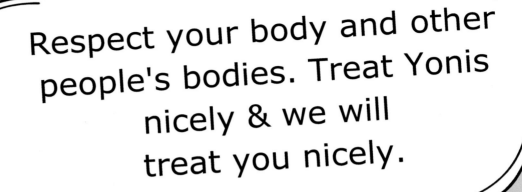

**Your vulva is yours to nurture, love, and learn about!**

It's perfectly normal and natural to touch your vulva in the privacy of your own room.* Remember, your vulva and entire Yoni is YOURS.

*To learn more about this, read my book
'Yoni Magic: What's the 'M' Word.'

Now that you know more about your anatomy, do you want to help me smash shame monsters?

Well, you've already started! Keep learning and honoring yourself and other peoples' bodies.

And if someone you know is spreading shame or making fun of you, **speak up** or find a trusted adult to help.

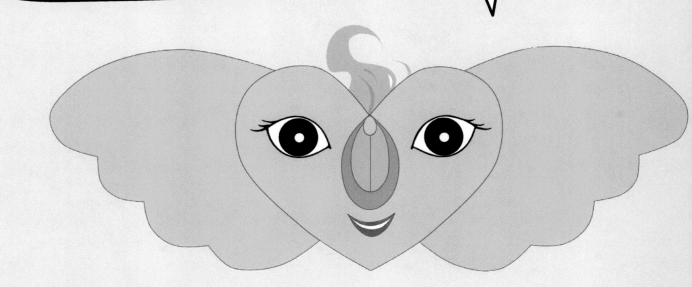

Together, we can break the cycle of shame and be proud of our bodies!

Life is full of changes & I'm here for you as you grow up.

Today we focused on the anatomy of Yonis - something that is important for everyone to understand, regardless of sex or gender.

For more information on assigned male anatomy, check out my book,
*Yoni Magic: The Spectacular Truth*

To learn about how babies are created read my book, *Yoni Magic: Creating Life.*

# Special Thanks to:

Dr. Debra Wickman
Dr. Julia Zigarelli
Cath Hakanson
Sophie
Julia Allison
Alexandria Wheeler
The Rooney Family
Whittney Lindsay
Casey Grooms - Elle Sakamoto
Leanne Hirsh
Soraya Elmaghraby
Angelina Coster
Dr. Afsoon Foorohar Kun
Taryn
Grace Chang
Sabrina Garcias

Made in the USA
Middletown, DE
10 January 2022

58301584R00020